ANTIGONE

by
Sophocles

Student Packet

Written by
Gloria Levine, M. A.

Contents:

2 Prereading Activities
2 Literary Analysis Activities
1 Study Guide (50 questions)
2 Vocabulary Activities
5 Critical Thinking/Problem Solving Activities
7 Writing Activities
1 Research Activity
1 Review Crossword
2 Comprehension Quizzes (levels I and II)*
2 Novel Tests (levels I and II)*

Plus   Detailed Answer Key

* Level II quiz and test are for students with advanced skills

---

Note

The text used to prepare this guide was the Dover Thrift Edition republished from a 1906 translation by Sir George Young. The page references may differ in other editions.

Please note: Please assess the appropriateness of this book for the age level and maturity of your students prior to reading and discussing it with your class.

ISBN 1-56137-745-7

To order, contact your local school supply store, or—

Child Graphics Company, LLC
PO Box 5612
Hilton Head, SC 29938-5612
800.543.4880 · FAX 843.671.4665
www.childgraphics.com

Name_____

Directions: With a partner, rate and discuss the following statements on a scale of 1–6. Keep these ratings in mind as you read *Antigone* and consider whether Sophocles—and various characters in his play—feel the same way you do.

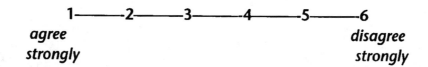

1——2——3——4——5——6
agree   *disagree*
strongly   *strongly*

Rating

_____ 1. Nothing is worth dying for.

_____ 2. You should obey the rules; they were made for a reason.

_____ 3. Do the honorable thing.

_____ 4. Life is hard.

_____ 5. In the end, most people get what they deserve.

_____ 6. What's past is past; get on with the present.

_____ 7. Children end up paying for their parents' mistakes.

_____ 8. Those who forget the past are condemned to repeat it.

_____ 9. It's never too late to learn from your mistakes.

_____ 10. You should do what is best for the "greater good"—not just for you and your family.

_____ 11. A wife should support her husband's decisions, regardless of whether she agrees.

_____ 12. Women should obey the men in power.

Name_____

Directions: Write a brief answer for each question. Use your answers for class discussion and to review for the quiz and final.

Pages 1-7

1. Where is the story set?

2. How did Antigone and Ismene's brothers die?

3. What order has Creon given regarding Polynices' body?

4. Why does Ismene tell her sister, "You are mad!" (page 2)?

5. What happened to Antigone's and Ismene's parents?

6. Why doesn't Ismene help her sister?

7. Who are the members of the Chorus?

8. When the Chorus members first appear (I.1., page 5) what background information do they provide?

9. Who was Capaneus (page 6) and what happened to him?

10. According to the Chorus, by whom were the seven captains overthrown?

11. Put the Chorus's advice into your own words: "Let us begin oblivion of the past" (page 7).

Pages 7-13

12. How can you tell the senators are puzzled by Creon's summons?

13. Briefly explain the line of succession that resulted in Creon's ascension to power.

14. According to Creon, how is he acting in the state's best interest by denying Polynices burial?

15. Why has Creon summoned the senators (page 9)?

16. Why is it that the sentinel "hastened—at my leisure" (page 10)?

17. What does the Senator mean when he says "This must be something more than natural" (page 11)?

18. What does Creon mean when he responds that "to say that guardian deities would care for this body, is intolerable" (page 12)?

19. Why is the Sentinel so happy to leave Creon (page 13)?

20. "He it is loves to range..." (page 13). Who is "he"?

Pages 13-22

21. Briefly summarize what the chorus is saying on page 14 (I.2) about man and nature.

22. How was Antigone captured—by whom?

23. What happened right before Antigone was detected alongside of the body?

24. What was Antigone doing with the "cruse" (page 17)?

25. Creon accuses Antigone of exulting in her outrageous deed (page 18). Cite one of her lines that demonstrates her exulting.

26. According to Antigone, why doesn't anyone express approval of her actions?

27. What does Antigone mean when she says "It was no bondman that perished, but a brother" (page 20)?

28. Why does Ismene say that she helped Antigone?

29. Why doesn't Creon order Ismene killed?

30. Why does Antigone accuse Creon of slighting his own son?

Pages 23-32

31. On page 23, what observations are made by the Chorus in I.1 and I.2?

32. Does Haemon support his father's decision to execute Antigone?

33. According to Haemon, do most people support his father's decision?

34. Why does Haemon mention trees on river banks (page 27) to his father?

35. Why does Haemon leave when Creon orders Antigone brought forth (page 29)?

36. How does Creon intend for Antigone to die?

37. Why does Antigone say she must marry Acheron? (page 30)

38. Why does Antigone mention Niobe's death? (page 31)

Pages 33-41

39. Who was Perseus and why does the Chorus mention him as Antigone is led to her death? (page 35)

40. Who is Tiresias?

41. What does Tiresias advise Creon to do?

42. What does Creon think of Tiresias' advice?

43. Tiresias predicts that Creon will pay for Antigone's death—how?

44. How does Creon change his plans after listening to Tiresias?

Pages 42-52

45. What is the gist of the Chorus' commentary on pages 42-43? What is their tone?

46. Why does the messenger say that Creon has lost all (page 44)?

47. How did Haemon die?

48. What was done with Polynices' body?

49. Whom does Creon blame for his son's death?

50. How does Eurydice die—and whom does Creon blame?

Name_____

Directions: A family tree showing the relationships between parents and children in *Oedipus the King* and *Antigone* has been started for you, below. Fill in the blanks as you read the play (= indicates marriage). You may want to use the extra space around the diagram to make notes about the characters and their actions.

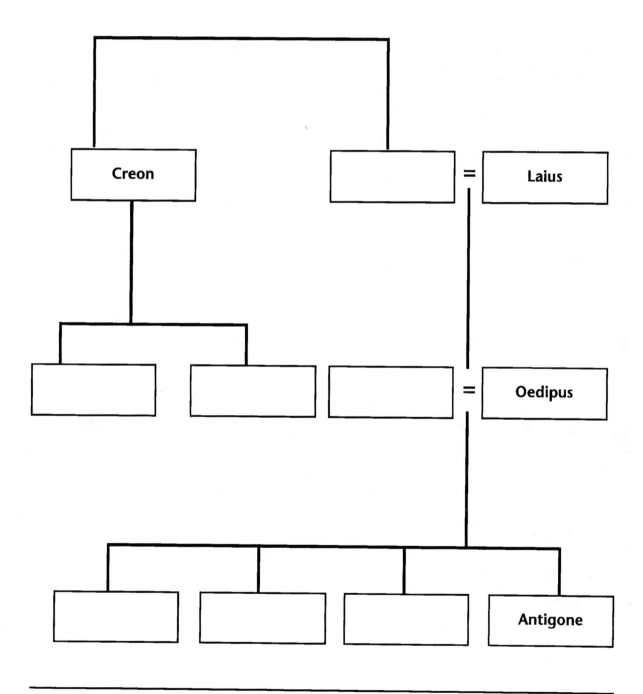

9

Directions: In **Column A** are mythical figures you will find mentioned in *Antigone.* Using a reference such as Edith Hamilton's *Mythology,* briefly explain the story behind each one. As you read the play, think about how the mythological figure is like Antigone and jot down similarities.

Mythological Character (add summary of story)	Is like Antigone because...
Niobe: _____ _____ _____ _____	_____ _____ _____ _____ _____ _____
Danae: _____ _____ _____ _____	_____ _____ _____ _____ _____ _____
Lycyrgus: _____ _____ _____ _____	_____ _____ _____ _____ _____ _____
Cleopatra: _____ _____ _____ _____	_____ _____ _____ _____ _____ _____

Name_____

Directions: Use the following sentence-starters for free-writing in your literature response journal.

1. When I feel that a rule is unfair...

2. The expression "Don't shoot the messenger"...

3. When your conscience tells you one thing, but ...

4. Getting punished for doing what you think is right...

5. When you try to fix a mistake and find it's too late...

6. Funeral rites...

7. Being very stubborn...

8. Dying for your beliefs...

9. Omens...

10. When a mother is torn between her husband and her child...

Name_____

The PSAT and SAT have several sentence completion items. This exercise will give you practice with sentence completions.

Directions: Complete the sentence by circling the letter of the word that best fits into the blank.

1. The man in the first row booed with _____ when Hava Biscotti, who had sung off-pitch, took his bows.
   (A) sepulchre   (B) pinion   (C) carrion
   (D) contumely   (E) piety

2. She lay in the tent listening to the _____ insects making their racket like creaky hinges in the muggy night.
   (A) strident   (B) tainted   (C) ephemeral
   (D) unwonted   (E) nether

3. When he _____ the will of the gods, he incurred their wrath.
   (A) transgressed   (B) relented   (C) desecrated
   (D) requited   (E) constrained

4. He vowed to spend his life helping others in _____ for his guilt.
   (A) scion   (B) anarchy   (C) expiation
   (D) augury   (E) reverence

5. In the animated film, a _____ of angels greeted the little dog at the gates of heaven.
   (A) discipline   (B) bale   (C) tenor
   (D) host   (E) gaggle

Name_____

The PSAT and SAT have several analogy items. This exercise will give you practice with analogies.

Directions: In each analogy question, you are given two words in boldfaced letters that are related in a specific way. You must figure out how they are related, and then select from the answer choices a pair of words that are related in the same way. Circle your answer.

Sample:

X. SPURIOUS : AUTHENTIC ::
   (A) DIFFIDENT : UNUSUAL
   (B) MASSIVE : PUNY
   (C) FELONIOUS : DISHONEST
   (D) AMPHIBIOUS : MOIST
   (E) ANOMALOUS : INCONGRUOUS

   Answer: (B)—Both pairs of words are antonyms.

1. **DORMANT : ACTIVE ::**
   (A) IMMURED : WALL ::
   (B) MOULDERING : CRUMBLING
   (C) HEINOUS : CRIME
   (D) KEENING : GRATING
   (E) COVERT : OVERT

2. **SEER : SOOTHSAYER ::**
   (A) CATACOMB : UNDERGROUND
   (B) LAVEMENT : WATER
   (C) FETTER : SHACKLE
   (D) BIER : CORPSE
   (E) WARD : STATE

3. **PRESAGE : PRESCIENCE ::**
   (A) DRILL : AUGURY
   (B) FORETELL : FOREKNOWLEDGE
   (C) REALM : TYRANNY
   (D) FABRICATE : SAW
   (E) EXPAND : ENMITY

4. **DEFILE : DESECRATE ::**
   (A) CLEAVE : APPEND
   (B) IMMURE : RELEASE
   (C) MANIFEST : PUBLISH
   (D) INTER : BURY
   (E) REVILE : INVIGORATE

5. **NOVICE : ROOKIE ::**
   (A) ORACLE : HISTORIAN
   (B) RILL : DECOY
   (C) STRAIT : BUFFOON
   (D) SHADE : PHANTOM
   (E) SPINDLE : WEAVER

Name_____

Directions: You are Haemon. You decide to write to a newspaper columnist about your fiancee, Antigone.

Step 1: Finish the letter begun for you, below:

Dear Gabby:

I am in love with a wonderful woman. The problem is that she and my father have decided to lock horns. It all started when _____

_____. Some people

say that Antigone has her faults—that she _____

_____—but I love her because

_____. Some people also

criticize my father for the way he_____

_____, but I love him, too. This situation is really tearing

me apart. What can I do?   **Signed,**

_____

Step 2: In small group, brainstorm possible advice Gabby might give to Haemon. Weigh the pros and cons of each suggestion. (A chart for organizing your ideas is shown below.) Then write a letter of advice back to Haemon, using details from the completed chart.

Choice #1: _____		What should Haemon do about the conflict between his father and his fiancee?	Choice #2: _____	
PROS	**CONS**		**PROS**	**CONS**

Character Sketch

*A **character sketch** is a brief, vivid description of a person. It includes physical characteristics —appearance, surroundings—and personality.*

Directions: Write a character sketch of Antigone (or Creon, or another character of your choice from *Antigone*). The finished sketch should bring that character to life for the reader.

Prewriting: *Get together in a small group to brainstorm a list of characteristics for Antigone (or another character you all choose to write about).*

- What does she look like? How would you describe her eyes? her face? her hair? Is she tall? short? What are her hands and feet like? Does she have any distinguishing marks? What does her usual facial expression tell you about her personality?
- How would you describe her posture? the way she moves?
- What is her voice like? How does she speak? What is her usual tone of voice—when speaking to Ismene? to Creon? to Haemon?
- How is she dressed? What does her clothing tell you about her personality?
- What other details about Antigone spring to mind? What responsibilities does she have? What does she like to do with her free time? What are her dreams and fears? How does she feel about herself?
- How do you imagine Antigone's family and background? What was her relationship with Haemon like when they were children? How does she feel about him now that he is dead?
- What words describe Antigone? What does she value? How does she feel about life?

Focus on the most "telling" details from your list. Which of the details will help you, the writer, convey a single, strong impression of what Antigone is like? Circle these.

Writing: *Choose one of the following ways to give the reader a single, focused impression of your character (approximately 250 words):*

a. Pretend that you are someone who knows Antigone well, such as Ismene or Haemon. Someone who doesn't know her has asked for your impression of her. Briefly tell what she is like, supporting your impression with details about her appearance, personality, and behavior.

b. Write a short story about Antigone. The story might focus on an incident that occurred when she was a teenager—before her father's rift with his two sons. The story should show how Antigone copes with a particular problem. Remember, the reader should come away from your story with a condensed impression of what Antigone is like.

Postwriting: *Read the character sketch aloud to your editing group. Make sure that it "sounds right." Is there a nice variety of long and short sentences? Do the words "flow" as you read the sketch aloud? Have you avoided unintentional repetition of words and phrases? Ask for suggestions about how to make the sequence of events more clear or how to give the reader a sharper picture of Antigone. Revise, rewrite, proofread, and publish.*

Writing Monologues

Project: Create a pair of **interior monologues** that reveal two characters' views of Antigone. Assume that your audience is composed of a group of high school students assigned *Antigone*.

Before Writing

1. Choose one of these pairs: Creon and his wife Eurydice, Haemon and Ismene, two Sentinels, two Senators, Tiresias and the boy who leads him.

2. Students who have selected the same pairs should discuss the characters' relationships with Antigone, then improvise conversations about Antigone.

3. After the improvisations, discuss ad-libbed lines that seemed particularly appropriate to the character or especially effective or insightful. Group members should suggest additional comments characters might have made.

During Writing: As you write your interior monologues, keep these questions in mind—

1. **Voice:** What am I like? How do I sound? What tone do I use? What sort of language do I use? What is my attitude toward my subject—Antigone?

2. **Audience:** Who is the reader? What help does the reader need to understand my thoughts?

3. **Purpose:** Why am I thinking about Antigone? How will I let the audience know the situation in which I am having these thoughts about Antigone? Am I arguing with myself about something? Am I trying to make a decision? to soothe myself? to enjoy my thoughts? to figure something out about myself or Antigone?

4. **Content:** Think about these questions—What is my relationship to Antigone? How did I meet her? How does she feel about me? How do I feel about her? What do I like about him? What don't I like? Does anything about her puzzle me? What do I think about the way she has been dealing with the death of her brothers? What values do we share? What differences do we have?

5. **Organization:** Which type of pattern should I use to organize my ideas— chronological? spatial? order of importance? comparison? a combination? Am I a clear, logical thinker? Or do my thoughts ramble? Do I have flashbacks? Do I ask myself questions? Do I hold conversations in my head? Do I joke with myself? Do I berate myself?

After Writing

Read (or submit for reading) your interior monologues to fellow students who have selected other pairs of characters for their monologues. Discuss and revise.

Name_____

Directions: (A) In small group talk about the relationships between the characters below. Label each arrow with a brief description of the relationship.

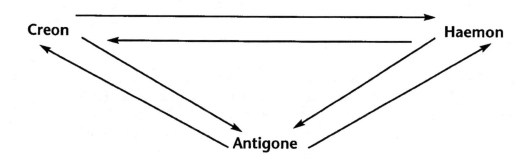

(B) Write an essay analyzing one of the relationships you have discussed. How do the two get along? What is the history of their relationship? What contributes to tensions between these two? jealousy? revenge? pride? different principles? Does the nature of the relationship change during the course of the play?

(C) Some critics have pointed out similarities between Creon and Antigone. Compare and contrast these two in class discussion. How are they similar and how are they different? in temperament? in their relations with peers? in their motivations? in their sense of religious duty? in their attitudes toward law and conscience? in their attitude toward Polynices? Fill in the Venn diagram, below.

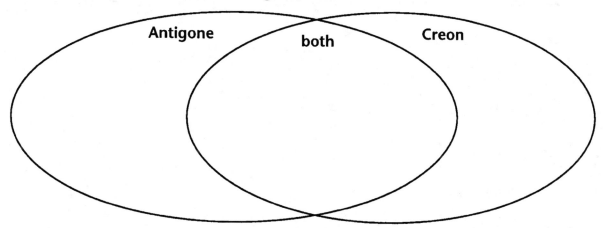

(D) Write an essay beginning with the following topic sentence: "Despite the central conflict between Antigone and Creon, they are similar in many ways..."

Satire

Directions: Many of the characters and events in *Antigone* have modern-day counterparts—in life, fiction, or art. For instance, you might see a similarity between Creon's part in the death of his prospective daughter-in-law and Saddam Hussein's role in the death of his own sons-in-law when they spoke in defiance of him (February, 1996). Do you see parallels between Sophocles' Chorus and today's media? Do the deaths of Haemon and Antigone—when they were on the verge of finding a happy ending—remind you of any recent movies you have seen? (If you're feeling creative, draw a cartoon that captures the Antigone-like nature of the present-day situation.)

Antigone	*Present Day Situation*	*Explanation of Similarity*
fratricide		
conflict between a political leader and relative(s)		
a "sign" that is ignored		
Creon's treatment of Polynice's body		
The Chorus' shifting sentiments		
The wife torn between her husband and son		
A woman who refuses to obey the men in power		
A tyrant who tries to intimidate his people		
An attempt to rectify a fatal error—too late		

Name_____

Character Motivation

Directions: Lawrence Kohlberg evolved a model of moral development to explain what motivates an individual to act as he or she does. Kohlberg believes that his model can be applied to individuals of any culture. There are six levels of moral development in his model. All people do not reach the highest levels. Decide which level best describes each character by the end of the play. Indicate your choice on the chart, and briefly explain the main reason(s) for your choice.

Level I	Acts to avoid pain or punishment.
Level II	Acts to get a reward.
Level III	Acts to gain approval.
Level IV	Acts because of belief in the law.
Level V	Acts for the welfare of others.
Level VI	Acts because of a self-formulated set of principles.

Character	Level	Reason for Choice
Antigone		
Ismene		
Creon		
Sentinel		
Haemon		
Eurydice		
Polynices		
Tiresias		

Name_____

Directions: Several characters in *Antigone* are faced with important decisions. Help them make these decisions by filling in decision-making grids like the one started for you below. Finish the chart below by adding another criteria question and another possible choice in the blank squares. Then make additional charts on separate paper for the other problems listed.

For each chart, list all of the choices you can think of and some criteria for measuring each choice. Then rate each choice by the "criteria" you list across the top of each chart (1=yes; 2=no; 3=maybe). Finally, choose one of the decisions and write an essay about the decision. (What was the decision? Why was it important? What choices did he have? Did she make the best decision? Why or why not?)

Problem #1: How should Antigone respond to the order for her brother's body to be left unburied?

		Criteria:		
Possible Choices ↓	Will I protect myself?	Am I being loyal to my brother?	Will this get anyone else in trouble?	
Obey the order and keep quiet.	1	2	2	
Complain to the Senators.				
Go to one of Ploynices' friends and ask for help.				

Problem #2: How should Haemon respond to his father's announced intention to execute his fiancée?

Problem #3: How should Creon respond to Tiresias' prediction?

Problem #4: What should Eurydice do when she learns her son is dead?

Writing Poetry

An **epitaph** is an inscription on a gravestone—sometimes in prose, often in poetry. Epitaphs in the form of poems are sometimes rhymed, sometimes unrhymed—often lofty, occasionally funny. Even the ancient Greeks apparently carved epitaphs into stone.

Project: Write an **epitaph** poem for Antigone.

First, read the following epitaph by Ben Jonson (English poet, 1573-1637) as a model for writing.

Epitaph on Elizabeth, L. H.

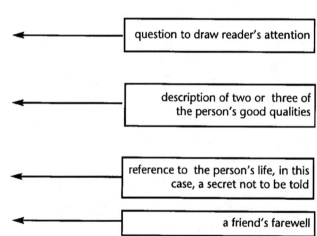

Wouldst thou hear what man can say
In a little? Reader, stay.
Underneath this stone doth lie
As much beauty as could die;
Which in life did harbor give
To more virtue than doth live.
If at all she had a fault,
Leave it buried in this vault.
One name was Elizabeth,
Th'other let it sleep with death;
Fitter, where it died to tell,
Than that it lived at all. Farewell.

question to draw reader's attention

description of two or three of the person's good qualities

reference to the person's life, in this case, a secret not to be told

a friend's farewell

- Now write a draft of an epitaph for Antigone, using as much or as little of Jonson's framework as you wish.

- Read the epitaph aloud.

- Expand and rewrite the epitaph. To help think of ideas to add, ask yourself— What else can I say about Antigone's good qualities? How did she improve the lives of others? Why will she be missed? What would Antigone think of this epitaph?

- Add rhyme, if you wish, and rewrite the epitaph once more.

- Add a simple design or picture that you would carve into the stone above the epitaph.

"This story just in. Eyewitness News has just learned..."

Project: Write the transcript for a TV news story about recent tragic events at the Royal Palace of Thebes.

1. Watch the evening news for ideas about how lead stories are presented, what key phrases are used by reporters, and what information is included.

2. Pretend that you are a TV reporter who has just been sent to the scene of three recent deaths—Antigone's, Haemon's, Eurydice's. Compose the report you will present on the 6:00 o'clock news about the shocking story, just breaking.

3. Decide on the most sensational of the recent events—the one you will use to capture the audience's interest. Write your key introductory phrase.

4. Jot down the key details about: Who? What? When? Where? Why?

5. Make up a list of three or four questions to ask witnesses at the scene.

6. Role-play your interviews with two or three eyewitnesses as well as another reporter on camera in the studio (other students who have read the play).

7. Consider how much background information your viewers will need to know about what has been going on at the Royal Palace. Jot down a list of events that preceded the killings—beginning with the death of Oedipus' father. Be sure to include the most lurid details—what Oedipus learned about his mother, his curse on his own sons, their fratricide, Creon's tyrannical edict, Antigone's defiance at the risk of death, Creon's treatment of the woman his son loves.

8. Summarize what has just happened—for viewers who tuned in late.

9. Insert some comments and questions from the news anchor in the studio.

10. End with questions that remain unanswered—with a promise to keep your viewers up-to-date. (For example, what will happen to Creon? What repercussions will these events have on those Greek citizens in the viewing area? Are the police pursuing anyone—or seeking additional witnesses?)

11. Write the transcript.

12. Read the transcript out loud. Fill in any gaps in key information. Change the order of details in your account to make the news item more interesting and coherent. Omit information that is repeated needlessly, but add repetition if it will emphasize an important point.

13. With a couple of other students (eyewitnesses plus the reporter(s) behind the desk in the studio), perform the news report in front of a real videocamera and record on tape.

DOWN

2. Daughter of Oedipus who defies Creon
5. Greek playwright who wrote *Antigone*
6. Creon's wife
7. Palace-setting of *Antigone*
9. *Antigone* has a ____ending.
10. Antigone's brother, killed by Polynices
12. Group of dancers and singers who comment on the action in Greek plays
13. Brother to Jocasta, successor to the throne
17. Haemon died by his own ___.
18. Creon ordered Antigone walled up in a _____.

ACROSS

1. The chorus is composed of _____ of Thebes.
3. He brought news of Antigone's disobedience to Creon.
4. Creon ordered this rebel's body left unburied.
7. Seer who predicted Haemon's death
8. Son of Creon, betrothed to Antigone
11. KIlling of brother by brother
14. Excessive pride and arrogance
15. Daughter of Oedipus, sister of Antigone
16. He killed his father and married his mother.
18. Eurydice ____ her husband before she died.

True/False: Mark each statement T or F.
(For 1 bonus point each, rewrite false statements on the back of the paper to make them true.)

___ 1. Oedipus was one of Antigone's brothers.
___ 2. Oedipus killed his father and married his mother.
___ 3. Creon killed Antigone's brother, Polynices.
___ 4. Ismene convinced Antigone to help her bury Polynices.
___ 5. Creon ordered that Antigone's brother, Eteocles, be given a proper burial.
___ 6. Antigone told Creon that Ismene helped her bury their brother.
___ 7. Antigone admitted to Creon that she knew of his order not to bury Polynices.
___ 8. The Chorus was supposed to be a group of Senators.
___ 9. Creon considered Polynices a traitor.
___ 10. The story is set in and around Athens, Greece.

Matching: Match each cause with its effect.

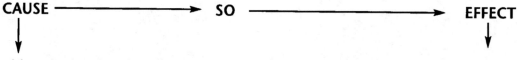

CAUSE ⟶ SO ⟶ EFFECT

___ 11. Antigone refused to be disloyal to her brother.

___ 12. Ismene believed that women had to obey the men in power.

___ 13. Polynices convinced Adrastus and others to take part in the invasion.

___ 14. Creon believed that Polynices wanted to lay waste to Thebes.

___ 15. Creon gave a death sentence.

a) She refused to help bury Polynices.
b) She would not allow his body to be burned.
c) She disobeyed Creon's order.
d) The seven leaders all died in combat at Thebes.
e) He denied his nephew the honor of a proper burial.
f) She agreed with Creon.
g) Ismene was horrified that he would tear his own son from the arms of his fiancée.

Fill-Ins: Fill in each blank with the word, number or phrase that makes the statement true.

As the story opens, Antigone is telling 1._____ of her plans

to 2._____. Antigone's 3. _____

tries to change her mind, reminding her that Creon will

4._____ _____.The Chorus, representing a

group of Theban 5._____, enters and describes the battle that ended with

the brothers' deaths. Creon is enraged by a sentinel's announcement that someone

has defied him by 6._____ _____. The

sentinel returns later with 7. _____, who boldly admits that she has

overstepped his law. When Creon orders 8._____ brought to him, she tries to

say that she 9._____bury her brother, but Antigone contradicts

her, saying, "You made your choice, to 10._____; I mine, to die."

Short Answer: Answer each question in a complete sentence or two.
11.   What happened to Antigone's mother and father?

12.   How did the two brothers die?

13.   Why did Creon order that one brother be buried properly—but not the other?

14.   Would you say that Antigone was "hard-hearted" toward her sister?

15.   Why does Antigone defy Creon?

Name_____

Unit Test • Level I
Objective

Identification: Find a character in the box who matches the description on the left. Write the letter of the character next to the matching number. Each character is to be used only once.

___	1.	Antigone's brother, killed by Polynices
___	2.	Antigone's father, married his mother
___	3.	Antigone's rebel brother; Creon ordered his body left unburied.
___	4.	Seer who angered Creon
___	5.	Group of senators from Thebes
___	6.	Creon's wife, killed herself
___	7.	Creon's son, killed himself
___	8.	Oedipus' daughter, killed herself
___	9.	Haemon's father, ordered Antigone walled in a cave
___	10.	Antigone's sister, afraid to defy Creon

A.	Antigone
B.	Ismene
C.	Polynices
D.	Eteocles
E.	Creon
F.	Oedipus
G.	Haemon
H.	Eurydice
I.	Tiresias
J.	Chorus

Multiple Choice: To the left of each item number, write the letter of the BEST response.

___ 11. Antigone's father Oedipus
A. was killed in the invasion of Thebes
B. killed both of his sons
C. killed his father and married his mother
D. was killed by one of Creon's assassins

___ 12. Antigone's brothers killed each other in a quarrel about
A. their sister Antigone
B. their inheritance
C. a woman they both wished to marry
D. who would rule the city

___ 13. Creon considered Polynices a
A. traitor
B. dupe
C. friend
D. patriot

___ 14. Creon forbade Polynices' burial because he wanted to
A. wait an appropriate length of time
B. punish the dead man by dishonoring him
C. halt his son's marriage plans
D. make sure his men were guarding the city gates

___ 15. Which is NOT a trait that Antigone demonstrates in her conversations
with her sister?
A. hardness
B. decisiveness
C. loyalty
D. conformity

___ 16. Which character provides some comic relief?
A. Haemon, when getting the bad news from Creon
B. the Sentinel, when delivering the bad news to Creon
C. Creon, when getting the bad news from Tiresias
D. Eurydice, when getting the bad news about Creon

___ 17. The chorus consists of
A. senators
B. messengers
C. guards
D. seers

___ 18. Which is NOT one of Antigone's reasons for defying Creon?
A. religious duty
B. sense of honor
C. love for her brother
D. ignorance of Creon's order

___ 19. Ismene does not help Antigone because Ismene
A. is in love with Haemon
B. disliked her brother
C. is afraid to die
D. dislikes her sister

___ 20. Which of the following describes Creon LEAST well?
A. stubborn
B. dishonest
C. power-loving
D. quick to suspect

___ 21. The seer suggests that
A. Creon should let Polynices be buried
B. Antigone is scheming against Creon
C. Creon should execute Antigone immediately
D. Creon should kill himself and die with dignity

___ 22. Which of the following describes Creon's reaction to the seer's words?
A. relief, then worry
B. rage, then acceptance
C. surprise, then sorrow
D. irritation, then suspicion

___ 23. Which of the following most likely expresses Antigone's thoughts about about hanging herself?
A. I'll make Haemon sorry.
B. I'll choose how and when I die, not Creon.
C. The thought of a long, slow death terrifies me.
D. I can't bear the guilt a moment longer.

___ 24. Which of the following might most likely be Haemon's final words?
A. I can't bear to live without you, Antigone.
B. I can't bear the guilt of knowing your death is my fault, Antigone.
C. If I can't have you, Antigone, I'll make sure no one can.
D. Father, forgive me for stabbing you.

___ 25. Creon's decision to release Antigone
A. was based on poor advice
B. angered Ismene
C. was overturned by the Senators
D. came too late

___ 26. The Chorus
         A. takes a leading part in the action
         B. displays a definite character
         C. refrains from commenting on the action
         D. changes in its sympathies

___ 27. When Antigone tells Creon, "It was no bondman perished, but a brother"
         she means
         A. The man who died may have been your nephew, but he was my
            brother.
         B. My brother died because he was bound to do what is right.
         C. It was a brother, not a slave, who died.
         D. It was a brother, not some tax collector, who died.

___ 28. When Creon says at the end, "O bear me, haste ye, spare not/To the ends of
         earth/More nothing than they who were not/In the hour of birth!" he means
         A. Take yourselves out of my sight. You who brought me this misfortune—I
            wish you had never been born.
         B. Hurry up and get far away from me; don't hang around idly babbling like
            infants
         C. Servants, take me away, out of the sight of men; I who am nothing more
            than nothing now.
         D. Take me away and kill me; I will offer no more resistance than a baby

___ 29. When Ismene says to Antigone, "At least announce it, then, to nobody, But
         keep it close, as I will" she means
         A. At least give no warning that you intend to disobey Creon; keep it quiet
            and I'll do the same.
         B. You may choose to disobey Creon, but I will not.
         C. I will help bury our brother nearby if you promise not to draw attention
            to what we have done.
         D. Don't tell anyone what you have done; I will get the word secretly to the
            one closest to your heart—Haemon.

___ 30. When Tiresias says to Creon, "Give place, then, in the presence of the dead. Wound not the life that's perished" he means
   A. Antigone has won. You may have killed her, but you can hurt her no longer.
   B. Enough people have died. Make room for Antigone in your heart and home.
   C. Do what the god of the underworld wants you to. You will die soon enough and have to face him then.
   D. Yield to the dead and bury Polynices. What use to kill the dead a second time?

___ 31. When Haemon says to Creon, "A city is no city/That is of one man only" he means
   A. You should rule as you see fit even if some citizens disagree with you.
   B. No city is property of a single man.
   C. Custom gives possession to the ruler of a city.
   D. If there were only one citizen left in the city, you would rule beautifully.

___ 32. Which is NOT an example of a force we see opposing Creon in the play?
   A. His wife criticizes his order not to bury Polynices.
   B. News arrives that someone has defied him.
   C. His son Haemon opposes him.
   D. The Chorus deserts him.

___ 33. When Eurydice learns of her son's death, she
   A. stabs herself to death
   B. hangs herself
   C. tries to stab Creon
   D. washes his body to prepare for burial

___ 34. When Creon learns of his son's death, he
   A. tries to stab himself
   B. declares bitterly that his son is better off now
   C. shouts that the death is all Tiresias' fault
   D. blames himself for causing his son's death

___ 35. In the end, Polynices is
   A. torn apart by birds and his remains cast into the sea
   B. never given funeral rites
   C. given a purifying bath and his remains are burned
   D. torn apart by dogs and his remains placed with Antigone's

___ 36. If Creon ran for U.S. president today, his campaign ads would most likely
A. be full of lies about what he plans to do
B. show him confidently pledging to do what he knows is best for his country
C. show him standing alongside his wife, promising voters they will get "two for the price of one"
D. contain clips from debates that reveal him to be unintelligent and irresponsible

___ 37. If Antigone were alive today, she would be best suited for a job as
A. a lawyer for the American Civil Liberties Union
B. a salesperson for Mary Kay Cosmetics
C. a kindergarten teacher
D. a corporate spy

___ 38. On the day of a family picnic, Ismene would probably be found
A. playing softball with the guys
B. locked in her room reading a good thriller
C. quietly cleaning up with the other women
D. arguing with her uncle about who should make the burgers

___ 39. Like Antigone, Creon
A. is easily swayed by the opinions of others
B. tries to be flexible
C. trusts his own judgment
D. believes in loyalty to family above all

___ 40. Antigone's burial of her brother is most like which action?
A. going over the speed limit because you are late
B. cooking the books to conceal money you have stolen
C. robbing graves for jewelry
D. engaging in a sit-in to protest defense spending

Fill-Ins: Fill in each blank with the word from the box that BEST completes the sentence.

catacomb	augury	carrion
anarchy	fratricide	blindness
thirteen	seven	patricide
hanging	stabbing	Fate

41. The killing of Polynices and Eteocles is an example of

_____.

42. Antigone did not want her brother's body to be stripped by dogs and birds in

search of _____.

43. Creon gave the order for Antigone to be imprisoned in a deep

_____.

44. Polynices led an invasion of Thebes in which _____ men each

attacked a different gate of the city.

45. Tiresias was frightened by the signs he observed when he went to his

accustomed place of _____ .

Name_____

Use separate paper for your answers.

Identification: Briefly identify each character or group in a sentence or two.
1. Antigone
2. Ismene
3. Polynices
4. Eteocles
5. Creon
6. Oedipus
7. Haemon
8. Eurydice
9. Tiresias
10. Chorus

Short Answer: Answer each question in a sentence or two.
11. What was Creon's order concerning Polynices and why did he give that order?
12. How was Antigone's reaction to Creon's edict different from Ismene's?
13. How does the scene where the sentinel announces that Creon's edict has been defied offer comic relief?
14. Who are the members of the Chorus and what function do they serve?
15. List three ways that Creon and Antigone are alike.
16. How did Creon change his mind about his order—and why?
17. Why do you think Antigone hanged herself?
18. How did Haemon die—and why?
19. How did Creon's decision to punish Antigone ultimately result in the deaths of his son and wife?
20. What was Creon's reaction to the deaths of his son and wife?
21. Creon told his son that he was doing what was best for the state. When Haemon replied, "A city is no city/That is of one man only" —what did he mean?
22. When Ismene said to Antigone, "At least announce it, then, to nobody, But keep it close, as I will"—what did she mean?
23. When Antigone told Creon, "It was no bondman perished, but a brother"— what did she mean?
24. Critics have pointed out that Antigone was not perfect. Describe what you see as one of her flaws.
25. What was the most tragic moment in the play, for you?

Essay

I. Analysis

Directions: Select A or B and write a well-developed essay of five paragraphs. Provide at least three clearly explained examples in support of your thesis.

A. Explain how Creon's arrogance contributes to several catastrophes. (What decisions does he make? Why? Who is hurt as a result?)

B. Write a character sketch of Antigone. (What are your impressions of her? How do you form these impressions? Why does she defy Creon? Why does she kill herself?)

II. Critical and Creative Thinking

Directions: Select C or D.

C. Defend or refute the following statement, using evidence from the play:

Antigone should really have been called *Creon.*
It is more his tragic story than hers.

D. Write three entries from the diary Antigone keeps. One entry should be written when she first learns of Creon's decree; one after she disobeys Creon; one shortly before she hangs herself.

Answer Key

Activity #1: Student opinion; answers will vary.

Study Questions

1. The story is set in the Royal Palace of Thebes (ancient Greece).
2. They killed each other in a struggle for power after Polynices led an invasion of Thebes.
3. He has ordered the body left in an open field, unburied.
4. Ismene thinks her sister is crazy to risk death by defying Creon's order.
5. Both are dead now. Their father Oedipus unknowingly killed his father and married his mother. When the truth came out, Oedipus blinded himself and Jocasta committed suicide.
6. Ismene does not want to die.
7. The Chorus is a group of Theban Senators.
8. They describe the invasion Polynices led after his brother cast him out of the city.
9. One of the invaders led by Polynices, all of whom were killed.
10. The Chorus says that Zeus overpowered these seven.
11. Forget the past and get on with the present.
12. They ask what he could want at this strange hour.
13. Creon was Oedipus's brother-in-law, next in line once Oedipus died.
14. Creon feels that while Eteocles was a patriot, Polynices was a traitor who deserves only condemnation.
15. He wants to announce that anyone who tries to bury Polynices will suffer death.
16. He was in no hurry to give his tyrannical leader the bad news that someone had tried to bury the body.
17. He implies that supernatural forces are at work here, since the culprit left no trace.
18. Creon is angered by the suggestion that the gods are not aligned with his decision about the body.
19. He didn't enjoy being the bearer of bad news—and facing Creon's anger.
20. The Chorus is commenting on the strangeness of Man, who crosses the sea even during winter's storms.
21. Man cleverly subdues all sorts of animals.
22. They found Antigone wailing and throwing dust on the body; when accused she denied nothing.
23. The guards swept the dust off the body. A wind blew up and when all was still, there was Antigone, wailing at the sight of the bare body.
24. She was giving the body a ritual bath from water in the container.
25. "Thus to me the pain is light to meet this fate."
26. They are afraid of angering Creon.

---

27. She is explaining that she must honor her brother, who was no "mere slave."
28. She wants to share the burden now that Creon is about to punish Antigone.
29. Antigone denies that Ismene helped bury the body.
30. Creon is sentencing the woman his son loves to death.
31. The Senators observe that once the gods are displeased, an entire family line suffers.
32. He is respectful at first, then grows angry.
33. He points out that many citizens are sympathetic with Antigone.
34. He is urging his father to be less inflexible, to bend like the trees..
35. Haemon won't give his father the satisfaction of making him watch Antigone die.
36. He intends for her to be left walled up in a cave.
37. She means that she must die (marry the river in the underworld).
38. She is comparing her suffering to that of Niobe, who was turned to stone for weeping over her murdered children;
39. He was the Thracians' king, Dryas' son, who was put in a prison of stone—as Antigone is about to be.
40. Tiresias is a blind seer who warns and angers Creon by pointing out that the gods are angry with him.
41. He advises him to release Antigone and bury Polynices.
42. He is angry at first, but quickly reflects on the wisdom Tiresias has always shown—and decides to take his advice.
43. Tiresias predicts that Creon will lose a child of his own.
44. He sets off with his servants to treat Polynices' body with honor and set his niece free.
45. The Senators pray joyfully for a Dionysian celebration of the healing of Thebes.
46. Now that Creon's son is dead, Creon's joy in life is gone.
47. Upset by Antigone's death, Haemon tried to stab his father, then fell on his own sword.
48. The servants gave the body a ritual bath and burned the remains.
49. Creon blames himself.
50. Eurydice stabs herself, her final words a curse on her husband. He blames himself.

Activity #2:

```
        Creon                           Jocasta = Laius
          |                                  |
   Menoeceus  Haemon            Jocasta = Oedipus
                                            |
                              Eteocles  Polynices  Ismene  Antigone
```

Activity #3: Like Antigone, all of these mythical women suffered—many punished in rocky tombs. Niobe was turned to stone for weeping over her murdered children; Danae was walled up by her father; Lycurgus was confined in a rocky prison for raging at Dionysus; Cleopatra had to deal with the blinding of her sons by the woman who hated her.

Activity #4: Personal response. Allow time for discussion of these entries before reading the play—and after the play is completed provide the opportunity for students to compare their responses with what they found in the text.

Activity #5: 1-D; 2-A; 3-A; 4-C; 5-D

Activity #6: 1-E; 2-C; 3-B; 4-D; 5-D;

Activities #7, 8, 9: Personal response. Provide the opportunity for "publication."

Activity #10: Answers will vary. Students should mention that Haemon respected his father, but was angered by his decision; Creon acted domineering toward his son, but loved him; Creon was enraged by Antigone because she—a woman—dared to defy him; Antigone was apparently in love with Haemon and uncowed by his father. Creon, like Antigone, was intelligent, responsible, determined to stick to his principles.

Activity #11: Personal Response

Activity #12: Answers will vary, but students should point out that Creon emphasized responsibility to follow the law while Antigone chose to obey a "higher law"—her conscience.

Activities #13, 14, 15: Personal Response.

Activity #16: Crossword solution on page 40.

Comprehension Quiz, Level I
True/False: 1-F; 2-T; 3-F; 4-F; 5-T; 6-F; 7-T; 8-T; 9-T; 10-F
Matching: 11-C; 12-A; 13-D 14-E; 15-G

Comprehension Quiz, Level II
Fill-Ins: 1-Ismene; 2-give their brother a proper burial; 3-sister; 4-kill any one who defies him; 5-Senators; 6-sprinkling dust on the body; 7-Antigone; 8-Ismene; 9-helped Antigone bury their brother; 10-live
Short Answer:
11.   Both have died. When Antigone's father realized that he had married his own mother, she killed herself and he blinded himself.

12. They killed each other in a battle over who should rule Thebes.
13. Eteocles was ruling when Polynices attacked; Creon considered the first a patriot and the second a traitor.
14. Some will agree that she is pretty rough on her sister when Ismene does not agree to help with the body.
15. Her conscience, religious duty, and love for her brother told her to honor him with a burial—at any cost.

Unit Test, Level I
Identification: 1-D; 2-F; 3-C; 4-I; 5-J; 6-H; 7-G; 8-A; 9-E; 10-B
Multiple Choice: 11-C; 12-D; 13-A; 14-B; 15-D; 16-B; 17-A; 18-D; 19-C; 20-B; 21-A; 22-B; 23-B; 24-A; 25-D; 26-D; 27-C; 28-C; 29-A; 30-D; 31-B; 32-A; 33-A; 34-D; 35-C; 36-B; 37-A; 38-C; 39-C; 40-D
Fill-Ins: 41-fratricide; 42-carrion; 43-catacomb; 44-seven; 45-augury

Unit Test, Level II
Identification:
1-Antigone is the proud daughter of Oedipus who defies her uncle's order and buries her brother, Polynices.
2-Ismene is Antigone's sister, who tries to dissuade her from ignoring the King's order.
3-Polynices is Antigone's brother, killed by their other brother in a struggle over supremacy in the city.
4-Eteocles is Antigone's other brother, considered a champion by Creon and given a proper burial.
5-Creon is brother to Jocasta, Antigone's uncle, the tyrannical successor to the throne.
6-Oedipus was Antigone's father, who set off a series of tragedies when he unknowingly killed his father and married his mother.
7-Haemon is Creon's son, betrothed to Antigone.
8-Eurydice is Creon's wife, who curses him and kills herself when she discovers her son's suicide.
9-Tiresias is the blind seer who angers Creon with his prophesy that Creon's edict will lead to catastrophe.
10-The Chorus is a group of Theban senators.

Short Answer:
11-Creon ordered that Polynices' body would be thrown out and left lying in the plain without a proper burial. He considered his nephew, who led an invasion of Thebes, an enemy of the city.
12-Antigone was defiant, declaring that the only honorable thing to do was to bury their brother. Ismene felt that they should lie low, obey the men, and protect their lives.
13-The prattling Sentinel is obviously reluctant to face his threatening, tyrannical leader. This lighter scene with the talkative guard follows the "heavy" pronouncement of Creon that anyone who defies him faces death.

14-The Chorus members, Theban Senators, comment on the action and provide transitions between scenes.

15-Both are stubborn, principled, determined to do what they consider right—and sometimes contemptuous.

16-Creon decided to release Antigone and bury Polynices because of Tiresias' dire prophesy.

17-She probably decided to die on her own terms—not Creon's.

18-He fell on his own sword in his distress over Antigone's death.

19-Antigone committed suicide rather than die a slow death in the cave—as prescribed by Creon. Haemon's suicide was a result of her death and Eurydice's suicide was a result of Haemon's death.

20-He lamented both, blamed himself, prayed frantically to die.

21-No city is the property of a single man.

22- At least give no warning that you intend to disobey Creon; keep it quiet and I'll do the same.

23-It was a brother, not a slave, who died.

24-Sample response: She could have been kinder to her sister.

25-Sample answer: Creon learns that he has lost both his son and his wife.

Essay

I. Analysis

A. Students might mention that Creon's tyrannical approach alienates or antagonizes several people: Antigone, Tiresias, Haemon, even the Senators. If he had been less inflexible in the beginning and allowed the burial, neither Antigone nor Haemon nor Eurydice would have died.

B. Students who choose B might provide evidence for Antigone's decisiveness, determination, loyalty, sense of religious duty, and courage.

II. Critical and Creative Thinking

C. Personal Response. (Those who agree with the statement might point out that Creon has more lines than Antigone and while her fate is sealed from the beginning—his spirals downward as the story unfolds. In the end, he has less to cling to than she. She dies knowing that she followed her conscience. He realizes his judgment was wrong, yet cannot escape through death.)

D. Personal response. These entries should convey her sense that she is honoring her brother and her gods—and her contempt for Creon.

Activity #16: Crossword Puzzle Solution